GARA

A Forgotten Oasis in Egypt's Western Desert

Mohamed Kenawi
and
Francesca Simi

Contents

Fig. 1. General view from Qasr al-Gamil over Gara and its lake.

Introduction

Many important archaeological sites and regions have been forgotten because of a paucity of information, neglect, and the physical difficulty of reaching them. Such is the case with the Gara Oasis, located in Egypt's Western Desert, forgotten for ages by the state's administration. And yet, because of Gara's geographical position, a study of the site is crucial to an understanding of the economy of the area both now and in the past.

The Egyptian authorities seem to have started continuous contact with its inhabitants only since 1983. Even so, that year, greater administrative attention was paid to Siwa, Gara's more extensive neighbouring oasis. That year marked a dramatic change in the life of the inhabitants of Gara, as they had to abandon the medieval Qasr ("fortress") and move away because of the heavy storms and rain that damaged a large part of the ancient settlement (figs. 1–2).

After 1983, Siwa underwent increased development. Investments were made in its spring water, attracting at first foreign tourists, and then Egyptian ones. These developments were triggered by an administrative decision aimed at promoting the oasis as a tourist destination. Changes included the laying out of asphalt roads, the implementation of electricity, and the addition of supplementary facilities year after year. The lives of the inhabitants also started to change. They adopted Arabic but kept using their own Amazigh language as well.

While Siwa Oasis underwent changes, the nearby Gara Oasis, representing the smallest living community in Egypt, did not attract the same attention. According to a former tribe leader (Sheikh Hassan), the province administrator of Marsa Matrouh asked the inhabitants, numbering 265 in 1983, to move to Siwa. They refused, preferring to live where they had lived since birth.

Geology and Geography

Gara is a small oasis located ca 110 km north of Siwa Oasis. The area was only connected by a paved road to Siwa in 2019. Today, Gara belongs to the Siwa District within Matrouh Governorate. Geographically the area is known as the Western Desert (which includes all the land west of the river Nile) and is part of the eastern end of the Sahara, also called the Libyan Desert. This area is characterised by rolling stone plateaus, sand sheets and dunes, a few elevations, and some depressions.

The Qattara Depression is the largest depression, comprising an area of 19,500 sq km with the lowest point at the altitude of -133 MSL (mean sea-level) (Sampsell 2003: 137). The Gara Oasis is one of the only two oases located in the Qattara Depression. The other, Moghra, is located at the north-eastern edge. The area today falls into a zone of hyper-aridity with around 8 mm of rainfall per year, according to the Siwa meteorological station. Because of this scarcity of rainfall, life is completely dependent on groundwater availability.

The Gara Oasis nestles isolated on a limestone plateau and is roughly 16 by 8 km. The lake of Gara, set in such a harsh desert landscape, is particularly stunning, with its outspread blue water, especially on its east, where the limestone plateau forms a steep cliff directly down to shore (figs. 3 and 4). At the water basin's western bank, the depression extends up to 4 km before meeting the plateau's cliff. The western bank of the lake is also characterised by the presence of several sandstone outcrops, many of which appear peculiarly mushroom-shaped (fig. 5).

The lake accumulates unused water from wells around the settlement and drainage from cultivation. None of the travellers visiting Gara in the past centuries has mentioned it. They probably avoided it. Nor is the lake visited by modern travellers.

The depression floor is also rich in natural springs and artesian wells (figs. 6–7). Consequently, this area is intensively cultivated with palms and other trees and plants. Agriculture is solely based on the spring's water. The lake itself is salty because the water table under the depression floor brings with it a high concentration of salt as it rises (Jackson 2002: 242).

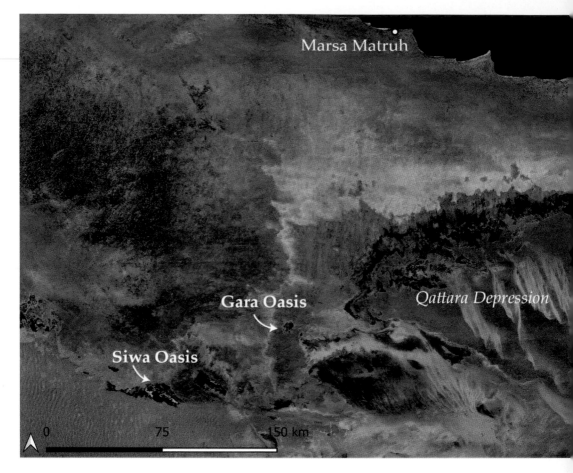

Fig. 2. Location of Gara and other sites mentioned in the text.

Gara: a Hidden Gem in the Desert

The toponym

There are different versions for the name of the oasis: *al-Gara*, which means 'the neighbour'; *qara* 'the hill'; *Garet al-Saghir*, 'the small neighbour'; and *Qaret al-Iskander* 'the hill (camp) of Alexander.' This small oasis was the only one that continued to be inhabited through the medieval period after the general abandonment of other oases around Siwa (e.g., al-Areg, Bahrein, Shiata, Sitra) (figs. 8–9).

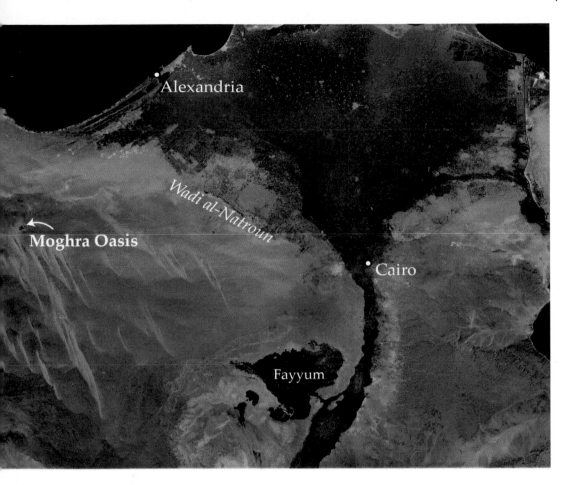

The smallest community in Egypt

The inhabitants of Gara Oasis are still the smallest independent community in Egypt. Today, they number around 640 individuals. They are members of the Amazigh tribe, direct descendants of the people who inhabited the fortified Qasr in 1983. Most inhabitants speak the Amazighi language and hardly any Arabic.

Prior to 1983, the inhabitants had not been provided with any education and healthcare and had no contact with the rest of the world. Subsequently, the Egyptian government started sending aid to the community. Once a year, doctors travel to Gara to offer basic health-checks and medical assistance. In 2003, the German state donated solar panels to the community, although these no longer function because of lack of maintenance. The Egyptian government therefore installed a generator to provide the community with electricity for the first time. The first large school was built between 2018 and 2019. The first asphalt road connecting Gara with Siwa was complete between 2019 and 2020,

Fig. 3. View of Gara Lake from the edge of the limestone plateau.

Fig. 4. The east shore of Gara Lake.

Fig. 5. The western fringe of Gara Oasis

Fig. 6. El-Qattara spring north-west of Gara Oasis.

Fig. 7. Hot spring, west of Gara Oasis.

but there is still little communication between the oases, aside from a single satellite phone used by the Gara community to contact Siwa in case of emergencies. A telephone system and other kinds of communication networks do not yet exist in Gara (fig. 9). The inhabitants have only recently started to use money. Families in Siwa and the few visitors that travel there usually carry a quantity of food that is then offered as a donation to the leader of the tribe. The leader then distributes the goods to the families of the tribe.

Gara in travellers's accounts

(N.B.: This section does not cover all the literature that mentions Gara, but focuses instead on the most significant references since the 1820s.)

In 1820, Mohamed Alia Pasha (ruler of Egypt between 1805 and 1849) sent 1300 soldiers under the direction of Hassan al-Shamshergi (governor of Beheira and leader of the military expedition to Siwa) to take control of Siwa Oasis. Alessandro Ricci, an Italian doctor and one of the pioneer travellers who visited Siwa and its surrounding area, records that the military expedition was composed of 3000 soldiers, while Ahmed Fakhry, an Egyptian archaeologist working mainly in the Western Desert, refers to 700 soldiers (Sammarco 1931: 555–70; Salvoldi 1931: 193; Fakhry 1944: 123). Both numbers may be correct, as Ricci mentions that the expedition marched with 4000 camels and that Arab tribes and their families joined it (Salvoldi 2018: 193). At first, the expedition took

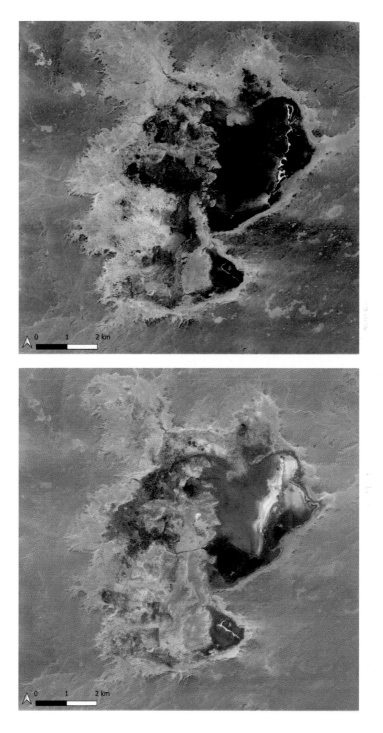

Fig. 8. Gara Oasis in two satellite images (above: Hexagon declassified satellite image (1974); below: modern Bing Map aerial view).

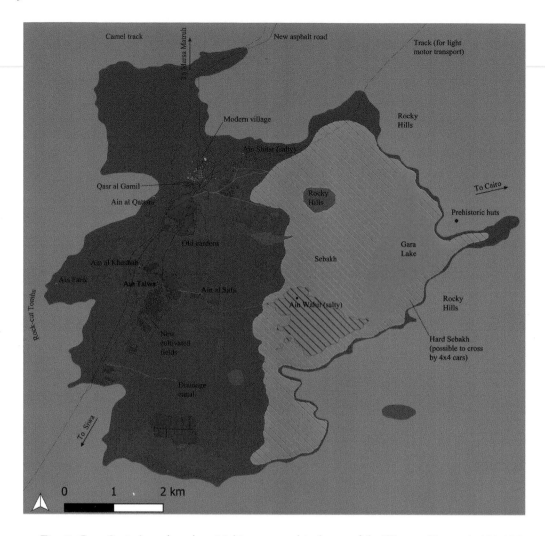

Fig. 9. Gara Oasis (map based on 1940s topographical map of the Western Desert 1: 100,000, sheets 14 and 15, overlapping the Hexagon image, 1974 and Google Earth image, 2020).

the coastal route, but it moved south before reaching Marsa Matrouh and passed through the Qattara Depression and Gara Oasis (el-Refaii 1932: 24). The expedition camped at Gara Oasis to refill their goatskin water-bags. They found that the entire fortified village at Gara was deserted, as the tribe had fled to join their relatives in Siwa (fig. 10).

Ricci travelled with his friends to Siwa and followed the military expedition. He purposefully delayed his departure for two days to avoid the overcrowding of soldiers at each of the route's water sources. He was accompanied by Bernardino Drovetti, an Italian antiquities collector and diplomat, Enelgildo Frediani, a traveller with military experience who joined the service of Mohamed Ali in 1817, and Louis Linant de Bellefonds, an explorer and the chief engineer of Egypt's public works between 1831 and 1869. This trip took over 54 days. Although other travellers like John Browne and Frederick Hornemann reached Siwa before Ricci, they could not access the fortified village.

Ricci travelled along the north coast until al-Hammam, then turned south and stopped at Moghra in the Qattara depression. He then camped and passed by Gara Oasis. The military had to pass by Gara to access a water source: the reason that Gara is the main stop between Siwa and the rest of Egypt. Ricci and the troops spent a night at Gara after reaching the fortified village. The inhabitants had fled from the military expedition a few days earlier. Ricci visited the deserted "small city" as he described it, writing as follows:

> *"…. in meno di mezz'ora l'avevamo tutta percorsa. E dessa [sic] edificata sopra una delle molte rocche esistenti in quella valle, ed è composta di circa ottanta case, piantate qua e là alla rinfusa, molto basse, e costruite con pezzi di pietra informi, malamente congiunti, e ricoperte di rami di palma: le più grandi sono di due piani, servendo il primo, cioè il terreno, per gli uomini, e per gli animali, ed il superiore per le raccolte, e per le provvisioni. Tutto questo fabbricato è circondato da deboli mura, con due porte……".*

> *"….in less than half an hour we had explored it all. It is built on one of the many rocky hills in that valley, and is made up of almost eighty houses. These are built here and there without order, all very low erected with shapeless pieces of stones, badly joined, and covered with branches of palm: the largest have two floors, the ground floor for humans and animals, the upper one for collecting goods as a storeroom. All these houses are surrounded by weak walls that have two doors…" (Salvoldi 2018: 197)*

Ricci recorded around 80 houses constructed with irregular stone blocks, poorly joined to each other and covered by roofs built with truncated palm trunks. This account may be the first to describe the medieval settlement of Qasr al-Gamil at Gara. The name of the Qasr is mentioned for the first time by Breccia, the second director of the Graeco-Roman Museum of Alexandria (Breccia 1932: 59).

In October 1896, Wilfred Jennings-Bramly, a British army captain who was surveying springs and wells in the Egyptian desert for the Royal Geographical Society, travelled from Cairo to Siwa taking the route from Wadi al-Natroun to Moghra and then Gara (Jennings-Bramly 1897: 597–608). On 26 September, Jennings-Bramly marched to Deir Beranus and then towards Siwa. He arrived at Gara on 7 October. His company included two servants and three camels. He described "Ghara" as a strange town built on the summit of a rock. When he reached the site, all the inhabitants had already retired within the Qasr's walls. As with every traditional Qasr settlement located in the middle of the desert, the gates were shut at sunset, and no one was allowed to leave or enter.

Jennings-Bramly mentions a high number of annoying mosquitoes that cause fever, probably malaria. Malaria was also mentioned by Ricci in the 1820s as a major cause of death in Siwa Oasis (Salvoldi 2018: 209). In the1980s, cases of malaria were detected at Gara after the first Egyptian doctors reached the small oasis (Kenawy, Beier, and el-Said 1986: 101–3).

Jennings-Bramly also records how awful the water from the well of Gara tasted. He had probably drunk from an ancient well whose water had become salty and polluted from a lack of maintenance. In fact, Ricci recounts drinking freshwater from the well located in the Qasr (Salvoldi 2018: 216). The well mentioned by Jennings-Bramley was intended for cultivation. The saltiness of the water may have been another reason for the decrease in the number of inhabitants, aside from the deadly fevers and lack of medical care.

On the way back to Cairo, Jenning-Bramly decided to travel through the Areg, Sitra, and Bahrein Oases. His guide was not impressed by his initiative and advised him to travel back to Cairo via the usual route through Gara, since this was the shortest and most common route for travellers. It probably was the traditional route until 1928, when King Fouad I of Egypt decided to travel using a "new" route. If that is correct, it is possible to suppose that, like most travellers, Alexander the Great crossed the Western Desert by passing through Gara and the Qattara Depression rather than via a theoretical route through Marsa Matrouh or the Bahariya Oasis when he travelled to the Amun Temple at Siwa in 332 BC (*Plutarch*, Life of Alexander, chapter 27; Arrian, *Anabasis*, Book 3,

Fig. 10. Drawing of Gara Oasis and the Qasr in 1820 by Louis Linant de Bellefonds.

chapters 3–4). On his map, in fact, Claudius Ptolemy, writing in the 2nd century AD, mentions two locations in Amun province: Siwa and the "camp of Alexander", a likely reference to Gara (*Geography*, Book 4, chapter 6).

Arthur White, a British administrator, geographer, and traveller, conducted a similar trip using the same Arab guides who had accompanied Jennings-Bramly on his trip (White 1899: 47). White left Deir Anba Makar and travelled towards Moghra. He then stopped by Ain Urua, where he did not find water, forcing him to travel faster in order to reach Gara oasis for freshwater. His actions strongly suggest that Gara was a crucial logistical stop and freshwater source in the middle of the desert. The trip from Moghra to Gara would have taken 6 days if they had travelled 8 hours per day, and it would then have taken 3 days to travel from Gara to Siwa. White mentions that around 75 people were living Gara and that there were two water wells (White 1899: 118) (fig. 11).

Oric Bates was an archaeologist and historian who passed by Gara in 1910 while conducting an expedition to Cyrene. Two of his photographs of Gara were published by the archaeologist Donald White (White 1998: 166). These might be the earliest photographs of the Qasr. One of them shows a caravan approaching Gara (fig. 12).

In 1927, the population of Gara numbered 100 inhabitants described as "the poor, slaves, and servants" by Hussein el-Refaii, commissioned to write a report about Siwa Oasis as part of a development plan for the Kingdom of Egypt (el-Refaii 1932: 30). In 1928, King Fouad I travelled to Siwa Oasis (Breccia 1929). His visit prompted the creation of a film documentary, and in 1931, the Geological Survey of Egypt prepared a photo album with an introduction that mentions Gara as Qara or Garet Um el Sughaiyar (al-Misriyah 1931: x). The album notes that "the water of all the wells in this oasis is so brackish that crops do not thrive". It is not clear how much time the surveyors spent at each oasis during their trip to test the water nor what the agricultural potential of the area might have been (figs. 13–15).

Fig. 13. View of Qasr al-Gamil (1930–1931).

Fig. 14. Qasr al-Gamil from the north, probably in the 1930s.

Fig. 15. Qasr al-Gamil (1994).

The Archaeology of Gara Oasis

The north-western edge of Egypt's Western Oasis

While Siwa is one of the less explored and understood oases of the Libyan Desert, despite being well known, Gara has been even more neglected by modern scholars. Its isolated position at the margin of the Qattara Depression and its apparent lack of outstanding archaeological remains are probably the reasons behind the lack of research on the area. And yet, this poorly investigated oasis may have had a crucial role as a logical crossroads for the north-south route connecting the coast with Siwa and its neighbouring smaller oases, as well as for the southwest-northeast route connecting Siwa and the northern fringe of the Great Sand Sea with the northern Nile valley and the Delta (fig. 16).

Even if little is known about Gara itself, it is still possible to put the oasis in a broader historical context thanks to what is known of other western oases (Fakhry 1973; Kuhlmann 1988; Bruhn 2011) and of the eastern Marmarica region (Vetter, Rieger, and Nicolay 2009; Rieger, Vetter, and Möller 2012; Vetter et al. 2013). All oases of the Western Desert have been inhabited, or at least frequented, since the Palaeolithic period between 90000 BC and 7000 BC. Around 5000 BC a process of aridification (Kuper and Kröpelin 2006) completely changed the entire Saharan landscape, forcing the migration of hunter-gatherers and pastoral nomads living in the Western Desert to move towards the Nile Valley.

Extensive contact between the Western Desert and the Nile Valley of the Pharaonic rulers started during the Old Kingdom period (2575–2150 BC) for political and military reasons. Nevertheless, because of the Western Desert's lack of natural resources and limited economic potential, and because of its hostile and harsh environment, this region – and especially the western and north-western oases – was never of interest to the political powers. The inhabitants of this region were and are still sometimes (in modern scientific literature) called "Libyans" or "*Tjehenu/Tjemehu*" (Rieger, Vetter, and Möller 2012: 159-61; Moreno Garcia 2018), a vague term used to identify non-Egyptian indigenous communities from different tribes, regions, and periods. These communities are largely sedentary, living permanently in the oases, but they also exploit the marginal desert area for livestock husbandry and pastoralism (Rieger et al. 2012).

Most of the oases had intensive contact with the Egyptians during Pharaonic times, although Siwa and possibly also Gara did not fall under Pharaonic rule until the 26th dynasty (664–525 BC) because of their remoteness. Even then, they maintained a degree of independence until Roman times. The Roman period is of particular significance for the oases, when they experienced significant demographic growth and agricultural expansion.

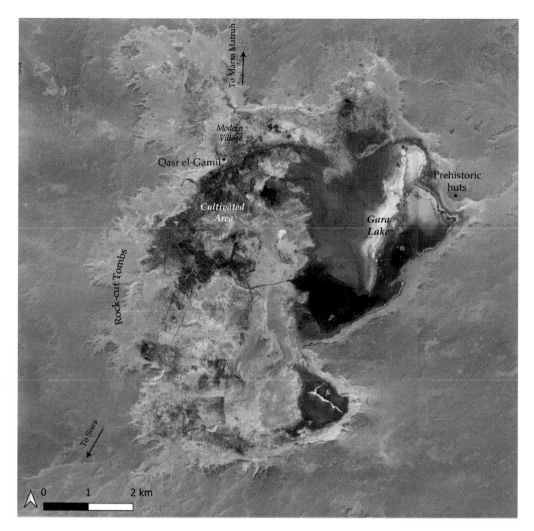

Fig 16. Map of Gara Oasis.

Qasr al-Gamil

In the ancient village of Gara, Qasr al-Gamil is the primary landmark of the oasis. The fortress is located in its northwestern sector, on a rocky hill at the border between the cultivated land and the desert (figs. 17–18). The Qasr has a semi-circular shape and is in good condition. It was inhabited until 1983. Some middle-aged inhabitants of Gara still easily recognise their houses in the Qasr and remember the circumstances in which they had to abandon them.

The walls of the fort are made up of houses, all built in *karshif*, a natural building material used in Siwa and Gara (figs. 19, 23–24). It is a mixture of mud, salt, and other minerals, sometimes with plant leaves added to the mixture. Qasr Shali in Siwa is also built of *karshif.* This construction material seems too weak to defend the fort, but there was probably no need for anything other than a high wall for protection.

The fort is organised around a marketplace and several houses that once had two to three storeys (figs. 20–21). There are also the ruins of a small mosque and a minaret. Different streets connect the districts of the village within the fort. A deep water well stands at its centre. This well was mainly used when the inhabitants could not leave the fort. The fort at Gara and the presence of such structures in Siwa (i.e., Aghurmi and Shali, two fortified villages in Siwa) suggest the continuous occupation of the oases during the last centuries, in contrast to oases that were abandoned and have no such structures.

Beneath the rocky hill, in the vicinity of the village, there are some simple rock-cut tombs (fig. 25). They possibly date to the Roman period and were reused for other purposes later (see below, p. 26). A simple Muslim cemetery is present on the western side of the hill. There are no surviving built tombs or tombstones except for the tomb

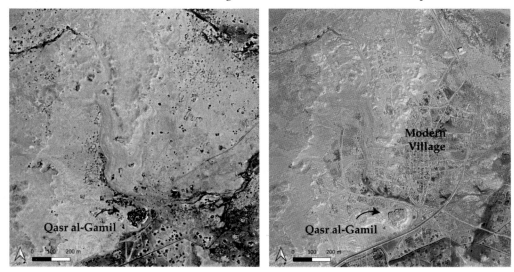

Fig. 17. Satellite maps showing Qasr al-Gamil (Hexagon image, 1974, left; Google Earth image, 2020, right).

Fig. 18. Qasr al-Gamil, January 2021.

Fig. 19. Qasr al-Gamil, remains of a two-storey domed house built with *karshif* and palm trees.

Fig. 20. Qasr al-Gamil, remains of two houses built along a main alley.

Fig. 21. Qasr al-Gamil, remains of houses and the marketplace.

Fig. 22. Qasr al-Gamil, the entrance.

Fig. 23. *Karshif* architecture at Qasr al-Gamil.   **Fig. 24.** *Karshif* architecture at Qasr al-Gamil.

Fig. 25. Possible Roman tombs within the rocky hill beneath the Qasr.

23

of a Sheikh (Sidi Yaga). One single-roomed structure, square and very plain, has been identified as a Sidi Yaga Mausoleum. A symbolic Muslim sarcophagus covered with a green flag stands in the middle of the room, and a row of ostrich eggs is attached to a rope hanging above it (figs. 26–27). Ostrich eggs are similarly used in a Sheikh's tomb in the Jaghbub Oasis in Libya. Ostriches used to be common in this region of the desert and have only recently completely disappeared (Wright 1997: 37–39).

The basic modern houses constructed by the government after 1983 are located on a flat plain north of the Qasr. The inhabitants of Gara practise no other activities in the oasis apart from cultivating food in limited fields. They simply tend to their livelihoods and basic needs.

Fig. 26. Gara, two monumental tombs, one in ruins, the other identified as the tomb of a Sheikh (Sidi Yaga).

Fig. 27. Gara, monumental tomb of Sheikh Yaga.

A Roman settlement at Gara?

In the 1930s, a complete funerary Roman life-size statue of a woman was retrieved from Gara and brought to the Graeco-Roman Museum in Alexandria (fig. 28). It is probably from a Roman funerary context. This is the only recorded archaeological find from Gara stored in a museum. It dates to the first half of the 3rd century AD. The find was documented as coming from "Kasr al-Gamil", the probable name of the fortified Qasr (Breccia 1932: 59). A Roman settlement may have occupied either the same location as the fortified Qasr at Gara or a location nearby, in the vicinity of a so-called "Roman well", in an area locals call the Roman "spring eye" (fig. 33).

Fig. 28. Roman statue found at Qasr al-Gamil, Gara in the 1930s.

The western section of Gara Oasis is characterised by the presence of several rock-cut tombs hewn into the vertical plateau cliffs or into numerous sandstone outcrops that are features of the area (figs. 29–32). The same outcrop where the old village of Gara was built also incorporates some rock-cut tombs, later reused as cellars by dwellers of Qarat Umm el-Sagheir. Such numerous and sparse features, a very common feature of many oases of the Western Desert, represent a wide and complex funerary landscape. These peculiar structures are generally dated from the Late Egyptian to the Graeco-Roman periods, between the 6th century BC and the 7th century AD. This type of tomb is well known from Siwa (Fakhry 1973; Jackson 2002: 243–55) and nearby smaller oases such as Girba, Shiata (Aldumairy 2005), al-Areg, and Bahrein (Fakhry 1973; Jackson 2002: 260), as well as Farafra (Boozer 2020: 159; Jackson 2002, 230–32), Dakhla (Gill 2016: 104–7) and Kharga (Rossi and Ahmed 2019). Further west in modern Libya, rock-cut tombs are also attested in the oasis of Jaghbub (Gill 2016: 422). Since similar rock-cut tombs have been identified and documented in Gara, it is possible to assign them also to the Roman period. Pottery sherds noted around some of these tombs might date to the Late Roman period (4th–7th century AD).

But where is the ancient settlement associated with this funerary landscape? Up until now, no such settlement has been identified at Gara either by travellers or by a recent remote survey using historical and modern satellite images. Based on the topography of the oasis, the logical location of a settlement should be on the west bank of the lake. In that case, the ancient settlement may be hidden by the modern cultivation of the area. A systematic and intensive survey of the entire western section of the oasis will be needed to identify the ancient settlement (fig. 33).

Fig. 29. Rock-cut tombs on the west bank of the oasis (group 1).

Fig. 30. Rock-cut tombs on the west bank of the oasis (group 2).

Fig. 31. Rock-cut tombs on the west bank of the oasis (group 3).

Fig. 32. Rock-cut tombs re-used by the inhabitants of Umm el-Sagheir.

Prehistoric huts on the eastern bank of the Gara Lake

The eastern bank of the Gara Lake completely lacks any rock-cut feature. The cliff in this part is very close to the shore of the lake, and sand covers the depression floor. However, on the plateau at the north-eastern corner of the oasis, an interesting archaeological site has been identified. Here, a prehistoric site was recognised on the top of the limestone plateau. A group consisting of at least nine clusters of circular stone structures takes a prominent position at the top of the plateau directly facing the lake (figs. 34–37).

The structures are very similar in dimension and construction techniques. For this reason and because of their spatial distribution, they are probably contemporary and belong to the same phase of the occupation. The site covers an area of ca. 3 hectares. The clusters are not regularly distributed but are spaced between 20 and 30 m apart. The structures are mostly located in areas cleared of stones and are characterised by the presence of one or two lines of slabs that create a sort of wall perimeter. The diameter of each structure is between 3 and 4 m.

Fig. 33. The so-called "Roman Well" immediately south of Qasr al-Gamil.

29

Similar structures are known from other oases in the Western Desert such as Farafra, Dakhla, and Kharga (Barich et al. 2012: 261–65); (McDonald 2009: 11–15). These sites feature circles of multiple limestone slabs and are generally dated to the Middle Holocene period, from the 7th and 6th millennia BC. They have been interpreted as prehistoric domestic huts. The presence of these dwellings near Gara testifies to the presence of a well-settled population at the limits of the oasis during the Middle Holocene period. An exploratory remote survey of the area using modern satellite images has revealed the presence of several other circular structures dispersed on the plateau at the eastern edge of the oasis.

Near these circular structures, two cairns have been identified (fig. 37). There are, however, no features by which it is possible to date these two structures. They may have had a funerary function.

Fig. 34. A cluster of three circular structures.

Fig. 35. Another cluster with clearance activities around the structures also visible.

Fig. 36. Another cluster of two structures.

Fig. 37. Two burial cairns in the vicinity of the group of circular structures (left: from the west; right: from the east).

Conclusions

The Gara Oasis represents an important missing link for an understanding of the archaeology of Egypt's Western Desert. Due to the strategic position of Gara at the intersection of several routes connecting the Western Desert with the Mediterranean Sea and the Nile Valley, many travellers had to pass by the small oasis. Alexander the Great himself probably passed through Gara in his way to the temple of God Amun in 332 BC Similarly, Mohamed Ali's 1820 expedition visited the Qattara Depression on their way to Siwa, passing by Gara.

Recent visits and remote sensing activities have revealed the presence of a multi-layered landscape comprising a possible prehistoric dwelling and an extensive funerary area, possibly of the Roman period. The little information available up until now and collected in this brief volume seems to vouch for the presence of several still unexplored heritage sites in this area. Only further research in Gara will unveil the forgotten story of such a unique oasis. A field survey is needed in the Qattara Depression to address the many unanswered questions.

Acknowledgements

We are grateful to Louise Bertini (American Research Center in Egypt), Bianca Badalucco (Regions in Flux Project), Luke Dady (Dorset Council), Charlotte McDurnan (National Trust, UK), Mariam Foum (American Research Center in Egypt), Salima Ikram (American University in Cairo), Giorgia Marchiori (Regions in Flux Project), Andy Reyes (Oxford University), Daniele Salvoldi (Arab Academy for Science and Technology), Norbert Schiller (Photographer), and Susan Walker (Oxford University). Thanks are also due to Nourhan Adel (independent researcher), Ali Kenawi (Siwa), Yasser Karakyiri (independent researcher), Eman Morgan (American University in Cairo), Amr Omar (American University in Cairo), and Mohamed Salah (independent researcher) for all the help and support we received. We want to thank in spirit the early explorers of the Western Desert who discovered new sites that have inspired us to visit Gara and its lake. Finally, we would like to thank the inhabitants of Gara Oasis who continue to live at the site, as they have done over centuries.

Bibliography

Aldumairy, A., *Siwa: Past and Present* (Yasso, Alexandria: 2005).

Barich, B. E., Lucarini, G., Gallinaro, M., and Hamdan, D. (2012), "Sheikh/Bir El Obeiyid: Evidence of Sedentism in the Northern Farafra Depression (Western Desert, Egypt)" in *Prehistory of Northeastern Africa: New Ideas and Discoveries*, eds. J. Kabaciński, M. Chlodnicki, and M. Kobusiewicz (Poznań, 2012), 255–78.

Boozer, A., "The Urbanisation of Egypt's Western Desert under Roman Rule" in *Urbanisation and State Formation in the Ancient Sahara and Beyond*, eds. M. Sterry and D. Mattingly (Cambridge, 2020), pp. 147–86.

Breccia, E., *Con sua maestá il re Fuad all' oasi di Ammone* (Cairo, 1929).

Breccia, E., "Fouilles et trouvailles: Mariout Inspectorat" in *Le Musée Gréco-Romain* 1925–1931 (Bergamo, 1932), 53–60.

Bruhn, K.-C., *"Kein Tempel der Pracht": Architektur und Geschichte des Tempels aus der Zeit des Amasis auf Aġūrmī = Ammoniaca* 1 (Wiesbaden, 2010).

Fakhry, A., *Siwa Oasis* (Cairo, 1973).

Fakhry, A., *Siwa Oasis: Its History and Antiquities* (Siwa, 1944).

Gill, J. C. R., *Dakhleh Oasis and the Western Desert of Egypt Under the Ptolemies* (= *The Dakhleh Oasis Project* 17) (Oxford, 2016).

Jackson, R. B., *At Empire's Edge: Exploring Rome's Egyptian Frontier* (New Haven, 2002).

Jennings-Bramly, W., "A Journey to Siwa in September and October, 1896", *The Geographical Journal* 10 (1897), 597–608.

Kenawy, M., Beier, J., and el-Said, S., "First Record of Malaria and Associated Anopheles in El Gara Oasis, Egypt", *Journal of the American Mosquito Control Association* 2 (1986), 101–3.

Kuhlmann, K. P., *Das Ammoneion: Archäologie, Geschichte und Kultpraxis des Orakels von Siwa* (Mainz, 1988).

Kuhlmann, K. P., "Roman and Byzantine Siwa: Developing a Latent Picture" in *Life on the Fringe: Living in the Southern Egyptian Deserts during the Roman and Early-Byzantine Periods*, ed. O. Kaper (Leiden, 1998), 159–80.

Kuper, R. and Kröpelin, S., "Climate-Controlled Holocene Occupation in the Sahara: Motor of Africa's Evolution", *Science* 313 (2006), 803–87.

McDonald, M. M. A., "Increased Sedentism in the Central Oases of the Egyptian Western Desert in the Early to Mid-Holocene: Evidence from the Peripheries", *African Archaeological Review* 26 (2009), 3–43.

McDonald, M. M. A., Wiseman, M. F., Kleindienst, M. R., Smith, J. R., Taylor, N., Wreschnig, A. J., Skinner, A. R., and Blackwell, B. A. B., "Did Middle Stone Age Khargan Peoples Leave Structural Features? 'Site J', The Forgotten Settlement of the 'Empty Desert', Kharga Oasis, Egypt: 1933 and 2011", *Journal of African Archaeology* 14 (2016), 155–79.

al-Misriyah, M. A., *Views of Typical Desert Scenery in Egypt* (Paris, 1931).

Moreno García, J. C.,"Elusive 'Libyans': Identities, Lifestyles and Mobile Populations in

NE Africa (Late 4th–Early 2nd Millennium BCE)", *Journal of Egyptian History* 11 (2018), 147–84.

el-Refaii, H. A., *Wahet Siwa: Men al-Nawahi al-Tarikhyia, al-Joughraphyia, al-Ijitimayeia, wa al-Iqtasadyia* (Cairo, 1932).

واحة سيوه: من النواحي التاريخية والجغرافية والاجتماعية والاقتصادية

Rieger, A.-K., Vetter, T., and Möller, H., "The Desert Dwellers of Marmarica, Western Desert" in *The History of the Peoples of the Eastern Desert*, eds. H. Barnard and K. Duistermaat (Los Angeles, 2012), 157–77.

Rossi, C. and Ahmed, M. I., "Filling the Gaps: Towards a Comprehensive List of Archaeological Sites in the Kharga Oasis, Egypt's Western Desert" in *Archaeology in Africa: Potentials and Perspectives on Laboratory and Fieldwork Research* (= *Arid Zone Archaeology* 8), eds. S. di Lernia and M. Gallinaro (Sesto Fiorentino, 2019), 89–100.

Salvoldi, D., ed., *From Siena to Nubia: Alessandro Ricci in Egypt and Sudan (1817–22)* (Cairo, 2018).

Sammarco, A., 1931, "Sull'inedito giornale di viaggio di Alessandro Ricci nell'Egitto e nelle regioni adicenti (1817–1822)", *Oriente Moderno* 11 (1931), 555–70.

Sampsell, B. M., *The Geology of Egypt: A Traveler's Handbook* (Cairo, 2003, rev. 2014).

Vetter, T., Rieger, A.-K., and Nicolay, A., "Ancient Rainwater Harvesting Systems in the North-Eastern Marmarica (North-Western Egypt)", *Libyan Studies* 40 (2009), 9–23.

Vetter, T., Rieger, A.-K., Klammer, O., and Möller, H., "Water Routes and Rangelands: Ancient Traffic and Grazing Infrastructure in the Marmarican Desert Areas (Northwestern Egypt)" in *Desert Road Archaeology in Ancient Egypt and Beyond* (= *Africa Praehistorica* 27), eds. F. Förster and H. Riemer (Cologne, 2013), 455–84.

White, A. S., *From Sphinx to Oracle: Through the Libyan Desert to the Oasis of Jupiter Ammon* (London, 1899).

White, D. "Stranger in a Strange Land: The Untold Story of the 1909 Bates Expedition to Cyrene", *Journal of the American Research Center in Egypt* 35 (1998), 163–78.

Wright, G. R. H., "Tombs at the Oasis of Jeghbub: An Exploration in 1955", *Libyan Studies* 28 (1997), 29–41.

Illustration credits

Design, typeset & photo editing by Vendi Jukić Buča
Manar al-Athar Booklet no. 5. Series editor: Andres Reyes
Published by Manar al-Athar, Oxford © 2022. ISBN 978-1-7396601-0-9
AEF Grant of the American Research Center in Egypt (ARCE)